Contents

Winter Wonderland 5
I Spy 6
Narcissus Moon 7
Khione restyles the Hamadryad 8
Playing knock a door run at Hecate's house 9
When Santa got stuck in a snowstorm... 10
Taste the Rainbow 11

WINTER WONDERLAND

When you tiptoe into the sugar
what will you spot in the distance?

Sugar is saying bye bye to the sky
and saying hello to the ground.

A peaceful forest is lit up by the proud moon
that is looking at itself in the pond
and making itself prouder.

Weary trees carry all their luggage of white snow,
branches bend and snap
because of the heavy blanket.
It offers them a cold biting chill
instead of a cosy cuddle.

A mysterious unknown cabin, looks lonely and sad
but brave enough to stand mysteriously
in the cold milky waves
that drop on the floor like freezing tears.

High above the cabin
Santa is flying in the bubbly storm
that attacks him.
He never wants grumpy children without presents
so he keeps on and on.

At last a swirling display begins killing the darkness
and turning it into a delightful rainbow.

What an amazing place we've been to!

*"When you tiptoe into the sugar
what will you spot in the distance?*

*Sugar is saying bye bye to the sky
and saying hello to the ground."*

I SPY

Ahead,
Atalanta is running,
her snow-crunch is loud
as she leaps and lands,
over frozen brooks and dodges
between trees.

Above,
Asteria of the stars,
waits near the crest
of the hill I can barely see
lost in the whirling
swirling white.

All around,
I can feel the breath of Boreas,
sender of the biting winds,
and Hemera,
primordial deity of daylight,
she is standing with me,
playing in the snow.

*"A peaceful forest is lit up by the proud moon
that is looking at itself in the pond
and making itself prouder."*

NARCISSUS MOON

Cast your eyes up moon
I'm here.
Lingering just at the edge
of the glittering pool.
Waters stilled,
a perfect mirror.
Your reflection captivates you,
entrances,
entices you closer,
invites you to sip –
slip even.

Watch your step moon,
cast up your eyes
and sit with me instead.

*"Weary trees carry all their luggage of white snow,
branches bend and snap
because of the heavy blanket.
It offers them a cold biting chill
instead of a cosy cuddle."*

KHIONE RESTYLES THE HAMADRYAD

Green is not your colour,
drop those silly leaves.
Muted brown is out of season, here,
try this – frosted shimmer, so much brighter.

White suits your frame,
hold this, and this, and this,
there, perfect.

Don't complain,
You look so much cooler now.

*"A mysterious unknown cabin, looks lonely and sad
but brave enough to stand mysteriously
in the cold milky waves
that drop on the floor like freezing tears."*

PLAYING KNOCK A DOOR RUN AT HECATE'S HOUSE

A cabin at a crossroads.
Noticed as we hike between trees.

The green door –
tempting.

We knock and leg it
shinning up a handy tree to watch.

The door creaks open.
No one looks out.

We hold our breath for so long we go dizzy,
the door snaps shut.

Confused, we slide down our tree,
sneak around the cabin,

a bubbling sound lures us to an open window
the smell of boiled cabbage.

A polecat appears at the crack, chittering
and the door snaps open.

"High above the cabin
Santa is flying in the bubbly storm
that attacks him.
He never wants grumpy children without presents
so he keeps on and on."

WHEN SANTA GOT STUCK IN A SNOWSTORM...

The sleigh is listing to the left,
three reindeer have broken free
and a nasty crack is snaking across the wood.

Santa is bailing fistfuls of snow
over the side,
like a sinking ship, but no use.

Tumbling from the sky,
each remaining reindeer kicks free
skitters off.

The sleigh hits the ground with a crack,
splits apart, spilling presents across the snow
and throwing Santa out into the forest.

He lands near a campfire,
a pack of white wolves raise hackles
and twins jump to their feet astonished.

Artemis stares at the man on the ground,
the broken sleigh, and lopes off in search of reindeer.
Apollo sighs, and offers Santa a lift in his sun chariot.

*"At last a swirling display begins killing the darkness
and turning it into a delightful rainbow.*

What an amazing place we've been to!"

TASTE THE RAINBOW

The sky splits
tumbling honey cakes to the ground
and a thousand colours
ricochet,
reflected by the snow
and darting like insects.

Iris, keeper of rainbows, golden winged,
appears, just for a moment,
winks at us
and blinks away.

Leaving us surrounded by cakes,
and light,
and the colours of the rainbow.

www.ingramcontent.com/pod-product-compliance
Lightning Source LLC
Chambersburg PA
CBHW041311110526
44590CB00028B/4328